MANAGING MENTAL HEALTH

Managing PANIC DISORDER

Katie Sharp

ReferencePoint
Press®

San Diego, CA

© 2022 ReferencePoint Press, Inc.
Printed in the United States

For more information, contact:
ReferencePoint Press, Inc.
PO Box 27779
San Diego, CA 92198
www.ReferencePointPress.com

LIBRARY OF CONGRESS CATALOGING-IN-PUBLICATION DATA

Names: Sharp, Katie John, author.
Title: Managing panic disorder / by Katie Sharp.
Description: San Diego, CA : ReferencePoint Press, Inc., 2022. | Series: Managing mental health | Includes bibliographical references and index.
Identifiers: LCCN 2021013119 (print) | LCCN 2021013120 (ebook) | ISBN 9781678201104 (library binding) | ISBN 9781678201111 (ebook)
Subjects: LCSH: Panic disorders--Juvenile literature. | Panic disorders--Treatment--Juvenile literature.
Classification: LCC RC535 .S534 2022 (print) | LCC RC535 (ebook) | DDC 616.85/223--dc23
LC record available at https://lccn.loc.gov/2021013119
LC ebook record available at https://lccn.loc.gov/2021013120

Contents

Panic in Mid-Flight

Kathleen was on a late-night flight home from Colombia, in South America. Flying alone, she woke up around three o'clock in the morning. She did not feel right. "I suddenly noticed how cold I was," she recalls. "Shaking actually. I noticed my hands were trembling. I tucked myself under my sweater and tried to take some deep breaths. It didn't help. I looked down to find my legs shaking terribly as well."[1]

She thought maybe she was having a seizure. She got up to go to the bathroom. She started to cry. "I felt like I had lost all control of my body, and I was embarrassed about asking a stranger to help me when I had no idea what was going on myself,"[2] she says.

When Kathleen left the bathroom, a flight attendant noticed that she did not look well. She summoned a doctor who happened to be on the flight. In addition to her fear and panic, Kathleen had to deal with everyone on the plane staring at her. "Thus, began a very public triage of my seemingly inexplicable symptoms,"[3] she says.

A Diagnosis of Panic Disorder

Kathleen was having a panic attack. But she did not know that at the time, and neither did the doctor on the airplane. After returning home, she had medical tests and exams that found nothing wrong. But the panic attacks kept happening. Kathleen had them on the streetcar on her way to work, at her office, and even at parties. And they always happened in public places.

After a lot of research, Kathleen eventually came to the conclusion that she was having panic attacks. She had always struggled with anxiety, but the symptoms had never been this bad. She admits:

> This was different. The lack of control I had over my physical response to anxiety left me feeling helpless. I couldn't commit to anything because I could end up in the throes of panic at any time. I missed events with friends because I was embarrassed to admit that I was struggling. I was physically and emotionally exhausted from pretending to be OK to avoid making others uncomfortable. I struggled to feel safe. And this kept me from fully living.[4]

Panic attacks like the one this airline passenger is experiencing are a common occurrence in people suffering from panic disorder.

The transition from having panic attacks to fearing panic attacks to the point of avoiding public outings and other normal daily activities to avoid them is the definition of panic disorder.

It took Kathleen months to admit she needed help. In addition to trying to overcome the stigma associated with mental illness, she faced other obstacles. The cost of health care can make it impossible for some people to get help—even with health insurance. Often the coverage for mental health treatment is not enough. If a person is unable to pay, they either go into debt trying to get help, learn to live with the condition, or take medication without consulting a health care provider.

In time, Kathleen found an affordable solution and worked with a therapist, who helped her recognize and cope with her anxiety and panic attacks. She says:

> Working with a therapist was immensely helpful. I was given practical tips for coping with panic when it arises and was able to learn to recognize my own physical cues of anxiety. But more important, I was validated. The seemingly incomprehensible way I was feeling was validated. It didn't have to make sense. It was valid because I was feeling it. I learned I could meet the immense fear I was feeling with compassion, and this often actually helped it subside.[5]

Hope with Treatment

Kathleen's story is not at all unusual for people with panic disorder. The first attack seems to come out of nowhere. The person feels a sudden and intense fear or discomfort that lasts a few minutes, maybe up to an hour. The fear or discomfort also brings on physical symptoms that can include a pounding or racing heartbeat, shortness of breath, chest pain, nausea, and a fear of losing control. The attack leaves the person feeling as though something is seriously wrong—like he or she is having a stroke or a heart attack or even facing imminent death.

Panic disorder can be quite frightening and worrisome. But as Kathleen found, once the condition is successfully diagnosed and treated, it is completely manageable, and a person with the disorder can live a normal, happy life. For most, that treatment includes psychotherapy—or "talk" therapy—and/or medication. In some cases, the medication can help people deal with the symptoms as they occur, while the therapy helps them build the knowledge, tools, and confidence they need to handle the next panic attack if and when it comes.

Chapter One

What Is Panic Disorder?

Many people with panic disorder have stories similar to Kathleen's. They may have experienced some general anxiety. They may have worried excessively at times about an exam or a personal relationship. They may have stressed about work or school or money. But then one day, seemingly out of nowhere, those feelings elevate to full-blown fear—of nothing in particular and for no specific reason. Their heart races, their palms sweat, they feel trapped and unable to move. With no warning or flashing sign announcing, "You're having a panic attack!," they are left feeling as though they are having a heart attack or a seizure or, worse, dying.

Then about ten to thirty minutes later—what can feel like a lifetime—the symptoms subside. The panic lessens, and they realize they are okay. After that moment of relief, they wonder what just happened and why. If in a public place, they look around and notice people staring at them. They may feel crazy. Some may head to the hospital to be sure there is nothing seriously wrong. And for many, the fear of having another attack, especially in a public place, starts to take hold, and their life takes a negative turn.

Katie knows she is not a laid-back, easygoing person. She can be a worrier and can get stressed out. But things started to get worse. She was feeling more and more stressed, crying for no apparent reason. Then one day at work, things got even worse. "I had my first SEVERE panic attack. Nothing happened. I was just at my desk replying to emails and then suddenly I felt myself losing it. It was like I just couldn't cope anymore with anything. I didn't know I was having a panic attack at the time—all I remember is feeling like I was going to die."[6]

> "I didn't know I was having a panic attack at the time—all I remember is feeling like I was going to die."[6]
>
> —Katie, a woman who has panic disorder

Fight-or-Flight Response

Feelings of fear and anxiety are the body's natural reaction to what it perceives as danger. These feelings tell us we could be in trouble, and they help the body prepare to deal with the threat. Scientists call this reaction the fight-or-flight response. It is something you have probably experienced many times.

To get an idea of what happens and what the fight-or-flight response feels like, imagine you are walking with your earbuds in place, happily listening to your latest favorite song. Your mind is elsewhere. Suddenly a fast-moving bicycle cuts in front you, catching you completely off guard. The bicycle and its rider are a danger to your well-being. If your body does not react, you are likely to get hit.

Luckily, your body's natural fight-or-flight response kicks in. It takes hold of your thoughts, your body, and your behavior. All at once your brain is no longer concentrating on your music but instead is focused on the bicycle and saving you from harm. Your body ramps up to take action: Your heart beats so fast you can feel it pounding in your chest. You breathe faster and heavier. Your palms sweat. You feel light-headed and full of fear. You might even feel like you want to throw up. All these changes prepare your body to do something, to protect you from the danger. Without any conscious input from you, your body jumps out of the way of the bicycle.

Your brain takes a second to process what just happened. You do a quick body check and are relieved you still have all your parts and pieces. But you can still feel the effects of the fear and the panic. It takes a few moments for your heart rate to return to normal and your body to calm down.

A patient who suffers from anxiety and panic attacks offers this description of how a panic attack can feel: "You know the feeling when you're rocking on the back legs of your chair and suddenly for a split second you think you're about to fall; that feeling in your chest? Imagine that split second feeling being frozen in time and lodged in your chest for hours/days, and imagine with it that sense of dread sticking around too, but sometimes you don't even know why."[7]

Panic attacks can happen in a public place, and the fear of that happening can take hold and make simple, everyday activities difficult.

Panic Attack Symptoms

This same thought-body-behavior reaction can happen even when there is no real danger to your well-being. You may have felt this fear or panic when you have been called to give a report in front of your classmates, a teacher asks you to stay after class, or the person you like is walking toward you. All these situations can cause your body to turn on the fight-or-flight response. Your heart races, your palms sweat, and you have a sort of out-of-body experience, unaware of what you are saying or doing. Again, your body is reacting to a real situation, ready to help you out—whether you need the help or not.

The body reacts in a very similar way during a panic attack. The difference is there is no obvious danger or reason for your body to want to fight or flee. You could be waiting for the bus, sitting in traffic, eating lunch, or maybe even sleeping. For most people, panic attacks happen suddenly and for no obvious reason. But the same fight-or-flight symptoms take hold. Usually they last about ten minutes, but no more than an hour, because the body cannot sustain that intense response any longer than that without becoming exhausted.

Angel remembers her first panic attack. She was going through a breakup and had just landed at an airport. "I was walking along and suddenly the lights seemed very bright and it seemed like there were an awful lot of people. I felt tiny and vulnerable, like any of those people could harm me if they wanted to. My knees turned to jelly immediately and I collapsed sobbing on the side of the corridor. I was hyperventilating and thought I was dying."[8]

Jenny was just nine years old when she had her first panic attack. Her teacher had asked her to go to the office to pick up some papers. Jenny says:

When I arrived there, a strange and terrifying sensation came over me, like I wasn't sure what I was doing. *Am I really here? Is this me or someone else I'm watching? Is this real?* I was freaked out, but managed to tell the woman at the desk what my teacher needed. I sat in a daze while she gathered the papers. It felt like the color had drained from my face and my body was numb. I hoped no one noticed that anything was wrong. There was no way I was going to tell anyone, it was too weird. I wouldn't have been able to describe it, and I assumed no one would understand. I rushed out of the office and felt better outside.[9]

Jenny had no idea what had happened to her. She just hoped those feelings would never come back. But they did. Then the fear of panic attacks took hold. And that is when panic attacks become panic disorder—when a person lives in fear of having more attacks and maybe goes so far as to change his or her life around to avoid being in public when the next panic attack happens.

Not everyone who has a panic attack develops panic disorder. Many people may have a panic attack or two and never have another one. Panic attacks can be a sign or symptom of other

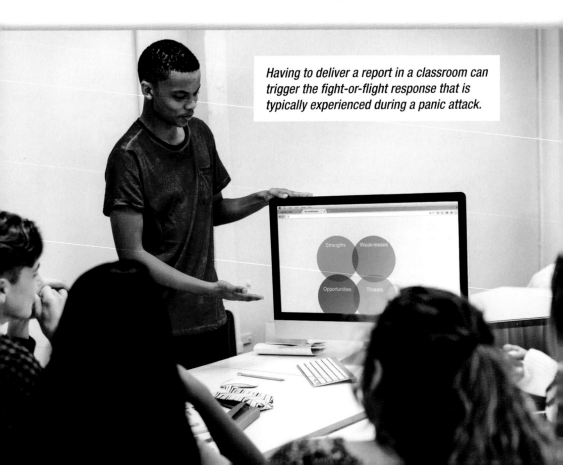

Having to deliver a report in a classroom can trigger the fight-or-flight response that is typically experienced during a panic attack.

More About Agoraphobia

About one out of every three people with panic disorder develops agoraphobia, or fear of places that might cause panic. This phobia is characterized by an intense fear of using public transportation, being in open spaces or enclosed spaces, standing in line or being in a crowd, and being outside of the home alone. People with agoraphobia will avoid these situations, often because they think being able to leave might be difficult or impossible in the event they have a panic attack. In the most severe cases of agoraphobia, a person can become homebound, refusing to ever leave his or her home. This behavior can cause significant problems in relationships with family, friends, coworkers, and partners.

anxiety disorders, including obsessive-compulsive disorder, post-traumatic stress disorder, and certain phobias.

The fifth edition of the *Diagnostic and Statistical Manual of Mental Disorders* (DSM-5), which health care providers use to assess and diagnose mental health disorders, defines panic attacks as

> an abrupt surge of intense fear or intense discomfort that reaches a peak within minutes and during which time four or more of the following symptoms occur: palpitations, pounding heart, or accelerated heart rate; sweating; trembling or shaking; sensations of shortness of breath or smothering; feeling of choking; chest pain or discomfort; nausea or abdominal distress; feeling dizzy, unsteady, lightheaded, or faint; derealization (feelings of unreality) or depersonalization (being detached from oneself); fear of losing control or "going crazy"; fear of dying; paresthesias (numbness or tingling sensation); chills or hot flushes.[10]

Jenny had more than four of the classic symptoms, including a pounding heart, light-headedness, dizziness, shakiness, a feeling like she was choking, vision problems, and the worry that she would have a heart attack. She also experienced derealization and depersonalization, two less common symptoms of panic disorder. Derealization is the feeling that a person is withdrawn from his or her surroundings—as if the world is not real. Depersonalization is like an out-of-body-experience in which a person feels separated from him- or herself. Jenny explains:

> The worst symptoms I've ever experienced weren't the physical ones. The scariest sensations were in my mind, when I felt like my brain was tricking me, teasing me that I didn't exist. . . . [I felt] detached from myself, like I was living in a fog or dream and didn't know whose body I was in. When I walked, it didn't feel like my legs were holding me up. My arms didn't feel like they belonged to me. I felt removed from the world and it was a struggle to bring myself back.[11]

More than Just Panic Attacks

The common symptoms of panic attacks by themselves do not constitute panic disorder. According to the DSM-5's definition of panic disorder, the panic attacks must be recurring and unexpected. In addition, at least one panic attack must be followed by a month or more of a persistent fear that more attacks—or at least some of their symptoms—will happen again. That fear must become so intense that the person alters his or her daily behaviors so as not to be caught in a situation where he or she cannot escape. The diagnosis of panic disorder also must rule out other causes for the panic attacks, such as drug use, a medical condition, or another mental disorder.

Mental health care providers recognize two different categories of panic attacks. Expected panic attacks are attacks for which there is an obvious cue

"The worst symptoms I've ever experienced weren't the physical ones. The scariest sensation were in my mind, when I felt like my brain was tricking me, teasing me that I didn't exist."[11]

—Jenny, a mental health blogger with panic disorder

or trigger. For example, people who are afraid to fly may panic if a flight is in their future—or they may avoid flying altogether for fear of having an attack and being unable to escape. This fear can cause a big problem if travel is part of a person's job. Unexpected panic attacks come out of nowhere, with no obvious cue or trigger.

Possibly the most debilitating characteristic of panic disorder is a fear of leaving home. In an effort to avoid future panic attacks, people with recurring panic attacks may significantly change their behavior and daily habits. They may avoid places and situations where attacks occurred in the past or where they worry they will feel trapped, such as on a subway, or will be humiliated by stares from strangers. When a person is unable to go to school, work, public places, and gatherings with family and friends, this avoidance can interfere with his or her ability to live a normal life.

This avoidance behavior may lead to agoraphobia, or a fear of public places, crowds, or being away from home. Panic disorder and agoraphobia sometimes occur together. Ellie has panic disorder with agoraphobia. She says, "Agoraphobia is exhausting. It stops us from doing the things we love. Because when you're scared of having a panic attack in public, you do the most logical

Agoraphobia, which sometimes accompanies panic disorder, can interfere with normal activities that involve being in crowds or public places.

thing you can. You stay away from the perceived danger. It feels easier and safer to just stay in your bed. On your own. Away from a dangerous world."[12]

Regarding panic attacks and panic disorder, it is important to understand that although many sufferers feel they may be dying, the attacks are not life threatening. The sensations are uncomfortable, and having a panic attack in public is often a cause for embarrassment. But the symptoms do subside, and they do not appear to have any long-lasting effect on the body. Regardless, when a person avoids living a normal life for fear of having a panic attack, diagnosis and treatment are absolutely necessary.

A lot of people have panic attacks each year. According to the National Institute of Mental Health, nearly 3 percent of US adults had panic disorder in the past year, and nearly 5 percent experience panic disorder at some point in their lives. According to the Cleveland Clinic, 11 percent of Americans have experienced a panic attack, and 2 to 3 percent go on to develop panic disorder. The condition is more common in females than males. Although it usually begins in the late teen years or in early adulthood, it may happen throughout adulthood and in childhood too.

Panic Disorder in Children and Teenagers

According to the National Institute of Mental Health, approximately 2.3 percent of adolescents have panic disorder. The symptoms in children and teenagers are not much different than those in adults. The main difference is that people in these age groups do not have the life experiences and knowledge to understand or express how they feel. Many have no idea what panic is and thus have no way to ask for help. This can make it difficult for the adults around them to figure out what is going on and offer help. This is especially true with teenagers because this is a time of many different emotions, with increased hormone levels, social pressures, and a full-time schedule of academics and other activities. Naturally, many teenagers can feel overwhelmed and anxious. For parents and other adults who do not know the

Panic amid a Pandemic

The recent COVID-19 pandemic led to heightened anxiety and possibly a dramatic increase in the number of people experiencing panic attacks. An analysis of Google search data before and after the World Health Organization declared COVID-19 a pandemic found a large increase in online searches related to anxiety, panic attacks, and treatments. Due to this uptick, researchers think that millions of people could have experienced panic attacks in response to the pandemic. According to the study, "People's search terms reflect relatively uncensored desires for information and thus lack many of the biases of traditional self-report surveys."

It may seem that people with panic disorder would breathe easier with stay-at-home orders, especially if they also have agoraphobia. But for some, the feeling of being trapped, unable to head to an emergency room or their therapist's office if they have a panic attack, has actually increased incidences of panic.

Those feelings are unlikely to just disappear once the pandemic ends. As the Kaiser Family Foundation points out, "History has shown that the mental health impact of disasters outlasts the physical impact, suggesting today's elevated mental health need will continue well beyond the coronavirus outbreak itself."

Barri Bronston-Tulane, "Google Shows Huge Panic Attack Rise During Covid," Futurity.com, September 22, 2020. www.futurity.org.

Quoted in Nirmita Panchal et al., "The Implications of COVID-19 for Mental Health and Substance Abuse," KFF, February 10, 2021. www.kff.org.

symptoms, it can be difficult to tell the difference between normal worry and panic disorder. But anxiety is more than overreacting or being dramatic.

Panic attacks can interfere with young people's relationships, schoolwork, and development. As with adults, children and teenagers may want to avoid situations in which they fear a panic attack may occur. They may not want to go to school or a friend's birthday party or even be away from their parents or guardians.

Without treatment, young people who experience panic attacks and panic disorder are at risk of developing severe depression. They also may be at risk for drug use or thoughts of suicide. However, early diagnosis and treatment can help prevent panic disorder from getting worse and interfering with daily life.

Chapter Two

What Causes Panic Attacks and Panic Disorder?

Panic attacks are defined by a long list of symptoms. But for each person, the experience of having a panic attack is very personal and unique. And it is always frightening and life disrupting.

An anonymous fifteen-year-old describes that first panic attack:

> I used to be a very chill go with the flow type of person but now it's hard not to feel overwhelmed by everything. My first panic attack was freaky. I didn't know what was happening. I was upset and then I got up to get something and boom. I couldn't breathe and then I started crying uncontrollably. . . . I kept thinking about things that were so irrational and it felt like I was going [to] cry. I don't know how long the attack was. I felt like it was forever, but then again it went by in a blink of an eye.[13]

A woman wrote about her first panic attack, which came on when she was shopping:

> Suddenly the lights seemed too bright, everything started to pulsate slightly and I felt really nauseated. I ended up falling to my knees and fainting in the mother-and-baby aisle of a pharmacy. . . . I had several "episodes" after that, but because they were so physiological I didn't [realize] they were panic attacks until my doctor diagnosed me with panic disorder. By then, though, I was deep in a spiral of anxiety and soon I couldn't leave the house without fainting.[14]

And another person describes what a panic attack feels like: "My heart feels like it's trying to push its way out of my chest and the world around me blurs. I often feel like I'm dying and it hurts to breathe. I sometimes hear a pulsing in my head, which seems to flow through my entire body. I always cry and need to pace around, which probably just makes it worse."[15]

The memory of the fear that overwhelms a person during a panic attack affects his or her emotional well-being and everyday life. Because having a panic attack can leave a person feeling out of control, he or she tends to become fearful and anxious about where and when the next panic attack will come.

Ella Henderson, a singer and former contestant on the TV show *The X Factor*, was suffering from anxiety at age twenty-five when she had a very public panic attack. "I was in [Los Angeles] and it happened in Ikea of all places. I honestly thought I was having a heart attack. And I just started shouting at this woman in front of me like, 'Help me! Help me!' and I don't really know what happened next. All I know is I woke up in a hospital on a drip and they told me I'd had a panic attack."[16]

"I don't know how long the attack was. I felt like it was forever, but then again it went by in a blink of an eye."[13]

—Anonymous, a fifteen-year-old who suffers from panic attacks

Henderson says that the terrifying experience turned her into a "hermit crab." She feared having similar attacks in public again. She says, "I could only do things from my own house and I could never be alone."[17]

What Causes People to Panic?

Scientists do not know exactly what causes panic attacks. They do not know whether the physical symptoms—the increased heart rate, shortness of breath, and sweaty palms—cause the fear or the fear causes the symptoms. The connection between fear and symptoms is being studied, as are other aspects of the disorder. The more scientists can understand about the hows and whys of panic attacks, the better able they are to develop and improve treatments and help people cope with their anxiety and fear. And when people with panic disorder can grasp what happens in their mind and body when panic strikes, they can start to feel a sense of control over the disorder.

> "When our defense mechanisms malfunction, this may result in an overexaggeration of the threat, leading to increased anxiety and, in extreme cases, panic."[18]
>
> —Dean Mobbs, a researcher at Columbia University

Scientists have not yet solved the mystery of panic attacks, but they do know that the brain and nervous system play a key role. The brain is the body's control center. The rest of the nervous system carries messages back and forth between the brain and the body.

Researchers have found that different parts of the brain play a role in causing fear and anxiety. They also know that the body's defense mechanisms (like running or freezing in the face of danger—the fight-or-flight response) are controlled by a deep region of the brain called the midbrain. When normal function is disrupted, this region of the brain might overreact, which in turn may trigger a panic attack. Dean Mobbs, a researcher at Columbia University who has studied the brain, writes, "When

our defense mechanisms malfunction, this may result in an over-exaggeration of the threat, leading to increased anxiety and, in extreme cases, panic."[18]

Another deep region of the brain, the hypothalamus, may also play a role in panic disorders. Researchers have found that stimulating the hypothalamus brings on the fear symptoms experienced during a panic attack. Normally, other areas of the brain keep these signals in check. But in panic disorder, if these other parts do not do their job, an overactivation of the deeper brain regions can follow.

Parts of the nervous system are also thought to be involved in panic attacks. One part, known as the sympathetic nervous system, is responsible for the body's response to stress. Another, known as the parasympathetic nervous system, keeps the basic functions of the body, such as digestion and heart rate, working as they should. According to Paul Li, a lecturer in

For many people with panic disorder, there are triggers that precede a panic attack. They know it is coming and can take steps to deal with it. But what about panic attacks that happen in the middle of the night? Researchers say up to 71 percent of people with daytime panic attacks have experienced at least one panic attack that woke them from their slumber.

The symptoms of nocturnal panic attacks are the same as daytime attacks: shortness of breath, sweating, and a feeling of impending doom. Nocturnal panic attacks can be more unsettling than daytime attacks, however. Because they begin when a person is sleeping, when that person wakes, they often feel groggy, disoriented, or frightened, and in the dark. Once the panic subsides, it can be difficult to go back to sleep, which then causes fatigue the next day. Ongoing worry about when the next nocturnal panic attack might strike can lead to insomnia and chronic fatigue.

People who experience nocturnal panic attacks are advised to establish a healthy bedtime routine. Keeping a regular sleep schedule, avoiding electronic screens before bedtime, engaging in relaxation exercises before bedtime, and avoiding alcohol and caffeine all might help prevent nocturnal panic attacks.

cognitive science at the University of California, Berkeley, these two play a role in panic attacks:

> When people feel stressed, their sympathetic nervous system typically revs up, releasing energy and preparing the body for action. Then the parasympathetic nervous system steps in, and the body stabilizes to a calmer state. If the parasympathetic nervous system is somehow unable to do its job, a person will remain fired up and may experience the heightened arousal characteristic of a panic attack.[19]

The Mind-Body Connection

Some researchers think panic attacks may happen when the brain misinterprets harmless internal sensations. People with panic disorder have higher levels of anxiety than those who do not have the disorder. This may make them more sensitive to the symptoms typical of a panic attack, such as an increased heart rate. This mind-body connection is called interoception, and it may cause people with panic disorder to perceive and react to problems that do not really exist.

Interoception is the awareness people have of signals the body gives off and the process by which the brain interprets those signals. Awareness of these sensations is why people experience feelings of hunger, fullness, thirst, pain, anxiety, frustration, and so on. Interoception also prompts them to take action in response to those signals. For example, when your stomach growls, that is a signal that you are hungry. So what do you do? You eat something. If you have goosebumps and start to shiver, those are signals that you are cold. So what do you do? You put on a sweatshirt or grab a blanket to warm up. A tight chest, racing heartbeat, and sweaty palms tell you that you are anxious and uncomfortable. So what do you do? You protect yourself from a possible threat.

Mental health professionals have been studying what happens when the brain misinterprets those types of internal sensations. This phenomenon, often referred to as interoception dysregulation, may play a role in depression and anxiety disorders, including panic disorder. For example, interoceptive dysregulation can cause a person to be overly sensitive to internal body signals. According to research that appeared in the *Harvard Review of Psychiatry*, "An individual with panic disorder may anticipate a bodily sensation such as heart rate increase and when this occurs in daily activities, such as exercise, the individual might interpret the heart rate increase as an impending panic attack." In other words, "What the individual experiences is in large part a reflection of what the brain predicts is going on inside the body,"[20] say the researchers.

Brain Chemicals

Other studies have found a possible link between panic disorder and naturally occurring chemicals in the brain called neurotransmitters. Hundreds of different neurotransmitters help communicate information between nerve cells in the brain. These chemicals affect how a person feels, thinks, and behaves. The neurotransmitter serotonin plays a role in mood, sleep, and appetite. Others include dopamine, which influences energy levels, attention, and movement, and norepinephrine, which is released in the fight-or-flight response. GABA, another neurotransmitter, influences excitement or agitation and feelings of calm and relaxation.

Because panic attacks are basically an overreactive fear response, researchers believe that a neurotransmitter imbalance may be involved in triggering them. For example, scientists have found that people with panic disorder often have reduced levels of serotonin. Because this neurotransmitter helps regulate anxiety and sadness, an imbalance can make a person more prone to both. If norepinephrine is out of balance, a person may have a more intense reaction to stress.

The bottom line is that researchers have not yet determined the exact cause of panic attacks and panic disorder. While they continue to research, they have come to some understanding of who is at risk for panic disorder.

Family History

Several factors can increase a person's risk for having panic attacks and developing panic disorder. Although studies connect these risk factors to the development of panic disorder, it does not necessarily follow that they cause the disorder. For example, more females than males tend to have panic disorder, but this does not mean being female causes it. Instead, risk factors for panic disorder are simply characteristics commonly seen in people who develop the disorder.

Panic disorder may run in families. According to researchers, having a close relative, such as a parent or sibling, with panic disorder puts a person at about a 43 percent increased risk of also having the disorder. However, scientists are not sure how it runs in families. According to psychiatrist Mohammed A. Memon,

Panic attacks and panic disorder are common mental health problems, so it is altogether possible that you could be with someone who has a panic attack at some point in your life. And there are things you can do to help. As you approach the person, remain calm. This will help reduce the person's feelings of panic.

Introduce yourself, and ask if you can help and, if so, what you can do. For example, ask if he or she would like to move to a quieter place. If he or she says no, do not push the issue. Be reassuring and listen without judgment.

Remind the person that he or she will be OK, that a panic attack is not dangerous and that it will pass. If the person is open to your help, try a technique called 5-4-3-2-1. Have the person identify and describe 5 things he or she can see; 4 things he or she can hear; 3 things he or she can feel/touch; 2 things he or she can smell; and 1 thing he or she can taste. This helps focus attention away from the thoughts and feelings that may make his or her panic worse. Above all else: Be patient with the person and stay until the panic attack ends.

"Although panic disorder is a disease with a significant genetic basis, the exact nature of the basis is unclear."[21]

As painful as it can be to realize the disorder might be passed down through a family, knowing that panic disorder runs in families can lead to an earlier diagnosis and treatment for people who experience symptoms. When Jenny's daughter Talee was young, Jenny recognized the symptoms from her own experiences with the disorder. Talee was diagnosed with panic disorder when she was just ten years old. "The last thing I wanted was for her to endure the same awful panic symptoms I'd suffered from—especially the derealization and depersonalization," Jenny says. "But sometimes when she had a panic attack, she'd say she didn't want to talk because it didn't sound like her voice. She couldn't explain it any clearer than that, but I knew exactly what she meant. That broke my heart."[22]

Stress and Anxiety

Stress is another risk factor for panic attacks. Major stressors such as losing a job, getting married, having a child, or being a victim of crime, abuse, or another traumatic event can put a person at risk. Kevin was ten years old when he had his first panic attack. He saw his uncle get hit in the head with a fast-moving baseball. Luckily his uncle was okay, but Kevin could not get the image he had seen that day out of his mind. While taking a bath that night, his heart started racing, his body felt numb, and he could not breathe. The panic attacks kept coming through his childhood and adult life.

Any major event—positive or negative—can bring on anxiety and a stress reaction. Even a happy occasion, like getting married, causes stress because it brings with it pressure and anxiety. Many stress out trying to live up to their own and others' expectations of a perfect wedding. Some people's brains may misinterpret the body's internal sensations of stress. These people feel these sensations—such as an elevated heart rate—and their brain may overreact, eventually bringing on a panic attack. What's more, if a person has a genetic predisposition to panic disorder, a stressful event may be the trigger that brings on the disorder.

People who suffer from anxiety or have an anxious personality are also at increased risk for panic disorder. Worry, distress, and fear are symptoms of anxiety. If the brain misinterprets the internal sensations of anxiety, it can lead to a panic attack.

Other Risk Factors

Problems with alcohol or other substances also can be a risk factor for panic attacks and panic disorder. These substances can cause a rise in heart rate or light-headedness, which can lead to feelings of panic and eventually a panic attack.

Smoking cigarettes also can put a person at higher risk. In fact, smokers are three times more likely than nonsmokers to have panic attacks and panic disorder. While many people smoke to feel more at ease in stressful situations, scientists believe that nicotine actually makes anxiety worse and can lead to panic attacks. This is because the anxiety actually comes back stronger once the nicotine wears off. "It's in their head that smoking is an effective way to manage their emotional distress, but it's probably only making them feel better because it's helping manage their nicotine withdrawal," says Brian Hitsman, associate professor of preventive medicine at Northwestern University. "Smoking actually increases your heart rate and causes changes in the body that are the opposite of relaxation."[23] The good news is that the risk of that first panic attack lowers in people who have quit smoking.

Caffeine intake is likely another risk factor for panic attacks and panic disorder. While many coffee drinkers enjoy a boost of energy and focus from caffeine, people who are at risk for anxiety disorders may not get this same positive effect. Instead, for them caffeine may trigger sweaty palms, a pounding heart, ringing in the ears—and sometimes a full-blown panic attack.

Although many people who drink coffee experience a boost in energy and focus, the caffeine can put an individual with an anxiety disorder at risk of a full-blown panic attack.

In fact, a study has shown that 400 to 480 milligrams of caffeine can bring on panic attacks in 35 to 48 percent of people who have panic disorder, while the same amount does not have that effect in those without the disorder. (A cup of coffee has about 94 milligrams of caffeine; a can of cola has about 40 milligrams.) Caffeine has several adverse effects on the body; it increases blood pressure and can cause irritability and insomnia. Sleeplessness due to caffeine intake can also increase anxiety and panic attacks.

Researchers will continue to look for the answers to what causes panic attacks and panic disorder. Clearly, there is no single cause. In most cases it is likely that several factors are at play. For example, a person with an inherited predisposition to the disorder might experience a traumatic event that brings on the first panic attack. That first attack may evolve into panic disorder. However, understanding what causes panic attacks and panic disorder and who is at greater risk for developing them can help mental health professionals and researchers work toward better treatments, and patients can make life choices to help them manage the disorder and take control of their lives.

Chapter Three

Managing Panic Disorder

Left untreated, panic disorder can lower a person's quality of life and lead to other mental health conditions, problems at home or school, and social isolation. For most people, seeking treatment can pave the way to managing and living with the disorder. Because everyone responds differently to treatment, it can take some people just weeks to see improvement, while others may need months or longer.

Too often there is a stigma attached to mental health problems. Many people with panic disorder feel they cannot ask for help or are afraid to reach out. They feel embarrassed. They think no one will believe them, or they worry people will think they are crazy. Some do not know where to turn for help, or they think treatment will not help them. But in many cases, once a person asks for help and follows a treatment plan, he or she looks back and wonders why it took so long to seek help. An anonymous person shares this story on the National Alliance on Mental Illness website: "I spent a lot of time suffering in silence. I never talked about my mental illness because I was so ashamed. I mean, I have a disorder that literally convinces me that I'm 'crazy.' Who wouldn't be scared to talk about that? But through lots of therapy, support from friends, and plenty of reflection, I am starting to truly believe that surviving panic disorder is something I can be proud of."[24]

Recognizing the Problem

In the past it could have taken months or years and lots of fear, isolation, and frustration before a person suffering from panic attacks could get an accurate diagnosis. Even today, with successful treatments available, people hesitate to tell anyone, even their doctors or loved ones, about their experiences with fear and anxiety. Instead, they suffer in silence. They distance themselves from friends, family, and others who could provide help. Some simply do not realize they have a real and highly treatable disorder.

One way to counter all this hesitation is with education. Once a person better understands the symptoms and discovers help is available, he or she can work with a mental health professional to find the treatment that will work best.

> "I am starting to truly believe that surviving panic disorder is something I can be proud of."[24]
>
> —Anonymous, a person who has panic disorder

For many people, the first step to recovery is to document the symptoms, circumstances, and timing of their panic attacks. Keeping track of when and where the attacks happen and the feelings and behaviors they bring can be helpful both in understanding what might be happening and in communicating with a health care provider.

Panic disorder is not like some other health problems—such as strep throat or diabetes—that have tried-and-true medical tests that a doctor can use to accurately diagnose the condition. Instead, a doctor or mental health professional considers the symptoms described by the individual, the frequency and severity of the attacks, the person's health history, and other criteria. One complicating factor of diagnosis is the similarity of symptoms between several mental health conditions. For example, people who suffer panic attacks only when they attend social events may have social anxiety disorder as opposed to panic disorder.

If and when a patient is diagnosed with panic disorder, the next step is to consider treatment options. The most common treatments are psychotherapy, medication, or a combination of the two.

Talk Therapy

Psychotherapy, often referred to as "talk therapy," is a treatment technique that mental health care providers use to help people identify and change emotions, thoughts, and behaviors that cause problems in their lives. The most common and successful psychotherapy for patients with panic disorder is cognitive behavioral therapy (CBT). This therapy teaches people different ways to think, behave, and react in situations that cause them anxiety and fear. CBT can help people learn and practice social skills, which can be key for treating the agoraphobia that often accompanies panic disorder.

Discussing one's symptoms with a therapist is an important step in finding the best treatment for panic disorder.

As its name suggests, CBT involves two types of therapy: cognitive therapy and behavior therapy. Cognitive therapy looks at how negative thoughts (cognitions) contribute to a person's fear and anxiety. Behavior therapy examines how a person behaves in situations that trigger anxiety. CBT for panic disorder focuses on understanding what triggers panic attacks and anxiety, forming healthier thinking patterns, and learning new behaviors to use when faced with fear and anxiety.

People with panic disorder tend to engage in catastrophic thinking. They often believe that the worst possible outcome will happen, no matter how unlikely that might be. CBT addresses these negative patterns with the idea that thoughts, not the environment, affect the way people feel. An event or the situation a person is in does not dictate the feelings that arise, but instead the person's perception of the situation brings about the fear, anxiety, and behaviors that lead to panic attacks.

According to the American Psychological Association, CBT is guided by these ideas:

Psychological problems are based, in part, on faulty or unhelpful ways of thinking.

Psychological problems are based, in part, on learned patterns of unhelpful behaviors.

People suffering from psychological problems can learn better ways of coping with them, thereby relieving their symptoms and being more effective in their lives.[25]

CBT providers work with panic disorder patients to help them, first, understand the thoughts, perceptions, and feelings that often precede a panic attack and then, second, change their thinking patterns to help them avoid the panic attacks. Successful therapy requires that patients be highly motivated and committed to treatment. It can be a very rewarding yet exhausting journey, but for many the benefits can be life changing. According to re-

When faced with a problem, most people want to do "something" to fix it. But for panic attacks, the best "something" people can do is nothing. Many people who have panic attacks do not know what triggers them. The fear and symptoms seem to come out of nowhere, they say. In actuality, they may stem from something going on inside the body. In clinical psychologist Michael Stein's, words, "Panic disorder is really anxiety about anxiety itself. It involves a fear of the internal bodily sensations that indicate that a panic attack might be about to start."

According to Stein, the best thing people can do when they feel a panic attack coming on is nothing. Easier said than done, of course, but practice helps. "Anything you do to try to fight or get rid of the panic will make it worse in the long run even if it makes you feel better. . . . The best thing to do with a feeling is to just feel it." By doing nothing about the panic and instead concentrating on something else, the brain learns that the internal signals are not a cause for panic or fear.

Michael Stein, "Why Your Panic Attacks May Seem Random but Aren't," *Understanding the Anxious Mind* (blog), *Psychology Today*, February 11, 2021. www.psychologytoday.com.

searchers Kristina Fenn and Majella Byrne, "CBT ultimately aims to teach patients to be their own therapist, by helping them to understand their current ways of thinking and behaving, and by equipping them with the tools to change their maladaptive cognitive and behavioral patterns."[26]

The goal of CBT is to identify and correct negative thoughts and beliefs. The idea is that if you change the way you think, you can change the way you feel. And if people with panic disorder can change the way they respond to the things they fear most, such as having a panic attack, they can learn to face that fear and begin to live a normal life. To achieve this goal, CBT employs education, restructuring of fear-based thoughts, and exposure therapy.

Common Strategies of CBT

CBT treatment begins with education. Many patients come to therapy with either no information or a lot of misinformation about their disorder. They may think that panic attacks can be fatal or are a symptom of insanity. They tend to feel embarrassed by their thoughts and behaviors. This is why education is so important. When patients learn about their disorder—that it is a medical condition and not a weakness—it helps reduce the shame and increase feelings of control.

Once patients understand their disorder, they can begin to work to restructure, or change, the thought patterns that bring on panic attacks and affect their ability to function. For example, if a patient is afraid to go to social gatherings, he or she might think, "If I go, no one will talk to me, I will feel stupid and anxious, and I'll have a panic attack and embarrass myself." This negative thought process feeds into the fear and anxiety that lead to a panic attack. Talking about these thought patterns with a therapist helps patients become more aware of them. Then patients can learn to restructure those thoughts so they do not lead to fear and panic.

Cognitive behavioral therapy (CBT) can bring relief from panic disorder by changing the way the patient thinks and feels.

Guided discovery is another strategy therapists use to help patients restructure their fear- and anxiety-provoking thoughts that can lead to panic attacks. According to researchers Aaron Beck and David Dozois, in guided discovery a therapist "asks a series of carefully sequenced questions to help define problems, assist in the identification of thoughts and beliefs, examine the meaning of events, or assess the ramifications of particular thoughts or behaviors."[27] The goal is to empower patients to discover things about themselves for themselves. For example, a therapist might ask a patient to describe the thoughts and feelings the patient has in a situation that the patient fears will cause a panic attack. After the patient responds, the therapist might repeat what the patient has said. Hearing his or her own thoughts aloud gives the patient a chance to listen to them from a different perspective and, hopefully, recognize why those thoughts are unhealthy and self-defeating. Once patients become more aware of their thoughts, together with the therapist they can learn to replace them with less anxious thinking.

Exposure therapy is another CBT strategy. Patients confront the objects, places, or situations they fear. According to the American Psychological Association:

> When people are fearful of something, they tend to avoid the feared objects, activities or situations. Although this avoidance might help reduce feelings of fear in the short term, over the long term it can make the fear become even worse. . . . In this form of therapy, psychologists create a safe environment in which to "expose" individuals to the things they fear and avoid. The exposure . . . in a safe environment helps reduce fear and decrease avoidance.[28]

One type of exposure therapy is called interoceptive exposure. In this therapy, the patient is exposed to the fears, cues, or triggers that cause the physical symptoms of a panic attack in order to defuse the fear associated with them. These symptoms are harmless in the long run but cause anxiety for the patient. In therapy,

What happens between cognitive behavioral therapy (CBT) sessions can be just as important as what happens during the sessions. Much to many patients' surprise, CBT practitioners often assign homework, which may include journaling and practicing breathing and meditation techniques. CBT journaling involves writing down internal experiences, thoughts, and feelings. Therapist Sarah D. Rees explains the benefits of journaling: "Just like talking, writing things down, getting them out of your head and down on paper, can be both freeing and healing. Venting in this way helps you make sense of things. Thoughts lose their power when we release them, so the intensity of difficult emotions is often reduced."

Homework, including journaling, can be the key to successful treatment. In fact, a review of studies on the benefits of doing homework while in CBT found that patients who completed these tasks at home generally had better results. This is because homework gives patients the opportunity to practice the new skills they have learned. Being able to apply these skills to everyday life increases the likelihood of successful treatment.

Sarah D. Rees, "What's the Link Between Journaling and CBT?," Sarah D. Rees—CBT Therapist, 2020. https://sarahdrees.co.uk.

the provider might have the patient engage in physical activity to raise the heart rate, a common symptom of panic attacks that can cause fear and anxiety. Over time, the patient learns that this sensation is not dangerous and is not something to be feared.

Patients who have gone through CBT say it brings real change. Dave had panic disorder for years. He finally sought therapy after a few of the worst attacks. His doctor suggested medication, but Dave wanted to try CBT. He says:

This type of therapy basically re-trained my brain not to "react" to the various triggers that set off my attacks, as well as learning how to control my body stress/tension to prevent a panic attack from getting out of control or even starting to begin with. . . . A key thing was to getting back to knowing what my body was supposed to feel like when it was in a "normal state" (i.e., healthy). . . . During an attack, I always felt like my body felt totally "out of balance."

. . . The "recovery" process took probably 2 years to get through, but I did make it! I can truly say that I have not had any panic attacks since.[29]

Drug Therapy

Medications are another option for treating panic disorder. Patients may use them alone or in combination with psychotherapy. When doctors prescribe medication for panic disorders, they most often prescribe classes of drugs called selective serotonin reuptake inhibitors (SSRIs) and serotonin norepinephrine reuptake inhibitors (SNRIs). These types of medications have been successful in treating panic disorder. They also have a low risk of serious side effects.

SSRIs include the drugs fluoxetine (brand name Prozac), paroxetine (Paxil and Pexeva), and sertraline (Zoloft). These drugs work by increasing the levels of serotonin in the brain. Recall that serotonin plays a role in mood, and scientists have found that people with panic disorder often have reduced levels of serotonin. SSRIs block the reabsorption (hence the word *reuptake*) of serotonin into nerve cells in the brain. By correcting the imbalance of serotonin in the brain, SSRIs decrease feelings of anxiety and improve mood, which in turn helps manage the symptoms of panic disorders. Different SSRIs are available to treat panic disorder, so if a patient does not do well with one, his or her doctor may switch to another one. Patience is key: these drugs can take weeks or longer before they are fully effective or for any side effects to lessen.

SNRIs are similar to SSRIs. They block the reabsorption of the serotonin in the brain, but they also block the reabsorption of another neurotransmitter, norepinephrine. A common SNRI for panic disorder is venlafaxine (brand name Effexor XR). As with SSRIs, the side effects with SNRIs are few and mild and usually go away after the first few weeks of treatment.

For some people, medication is the key to reclaiming a life free from fear and anxiety. For example, Elli had suffered from panic

attacks and general anxiety off and on from the time she was a little girl. She often felt happy, but underneath that happiness she was hiding a constant feeling of dread, helplessness, and shame about her fears and anxiety. She joined the cross-country team in high school, and running dramatically changed her mental health. She made it through college feeling much better. But within a year of graduation, the anxiety came back. Elli tried therapy, but it did not help. When the anxiety began interfering with her relationships, she saw another psychiatrist. Elli says:

> He didn't ask me to continuously discuss my feelings. (At this point the last thing I wanted to do was rehash what I'd never been able to understand.) Instead, he matter-of-factly asked me to describe my anxiety. He didn't treat me like a person who wasn't trying hard enough. He explained that brains are wired differently in each person and that this persistent anxiety was not my fault. . . .

Ultimately we agreed to try a low dose of medication—
something I had resisted for so long and continued to be
wary of. But just one month later, I got my life back. . . .
On this medication, the cloud was lifted. . . . Four years
later, I am still on the same low dose, and I am grateful
every day for this medication.[30]

Recent Research on Treatment

Researchers continue to improve existing treatments and develop
new and better treatments for panic disorder. For example, a study
in Sweden found that psychotherapy may be better than drug
therapy in the long run for people who have panic disorder. What's
more, the researchers found that unlike therapy for other disorders, therapy for panic disorder does not take years to be effective.
These researchers studied patients for over ten years and found
that 70 percent clearly improved and 45 percent were symptom-
free two years after completing treatment.

In another study, psychotherapy was
found to be more effective than medications, because therapy treats more
than just the symptoms of the disorder.
Therapy can help patients realize the
causes of their anxiety and fear; learn
how to relax; look at situations in new,
less frightening ways; and develop better coping and problem-solving skills.
Therapy gives patients the tools they
need to overcome panic disorder and
teaches them how to use these tools.

> "On this medication, the cloud
> was lifted. . . . Four years later,
> I am still on the same low
> dose, and I am grateful every
> day for this medication."[30]
>
> —Elli, a writer and editor who chose
> medication to treat her anxiety

For patients with panic disorder, there is no one treatment path
that will fit each and every person. The road to recovery involves
getting an accurate diagnosis and committing to doing the work it
takes to uncover the treatment that best suits a patient's particular
symptoms, circumstances, lifestyle, and more.

Chapter Four

Living with Panic Disorder

Living with panic disorder—the fear and anxiety of having a panic attack—can affect all parts of a person's life. One day everything is going along fine, and the next is filled with the sensations of panic. Perhaps a panic attack happened at the grocery store, a movie theater, or the train on the way to work. Suddenly that place—a place that once felt normal and safe—no longer feels safe. People who have panic disorder tend to avoid places where a panic attack happened. Now going to the grocery store is a problem. Going to the movies is not possible. And finding a new way to get to work is a necessity. Some people may even say no to any and every experience that may trigger a panic attack. But avoiding these places only increases and perpetuates the fear and anxiety.

Fortunately, there are effective treatments that can help people get their fear and anxiety under control. But treatment can take time for some, and treatment is not a cure. People with panic disorder are at risk of having a panic attack at any time, even if they have been through treatment. That is why learning to live with panic disorder is their only shot at a normal life.

Through treatment, people with panic disorder learn they cannot control panic attacks. In fact, the harder they try to control them, the worse they may get. Instead, it takes education, time, and practice to manage the attacks. Debra Kissen, a clinical psychologist who specializes in CBT and also suffered from panic disorder, says, "I know it is possible to arrive at a place where you can experience panic and anxiety as nothing more than a brain blip. You can get to a place where you are able to observe vs. get lost in your panic." She offers these reminders, which can empower a person with panic disorder to manage the fear:

> Panic is a false alarm going off in your brain.
>
> Just because you feel like you are in danger does not mean you are truly in danger.
>
> Struggling with panic does not make you weak or broken; it just makes you a run-of-the-mill flawed human (like the rest of us).
>
> The way past panic is to face it head on. You can teach your brain that you aren't actually in danger by staying put and riding out the panic wave.
>
> You can handle panic! It is not dangerous, it is just super-duper uncomfortable.[31]

People with panic disorder have more resources and techniques available than ever before. Learning what works and what does not is part of the journey. In addition to the more mainstream treatments, patients can use other tools to take control of their disorder and their life. Seeking professional treatment is always the best way to cope with panic disorder. But there are other things people can do along with therapy and/or medication to cope with panic attacks.

"Struggling with panic does not make you weak or broken."[31]

—Debra Kissen, a clinical psychologist who specializes in CBT and also suffered from panic disorder

Exercise

Exercise is good for the body. Among other things, it can keep weight in check, is good for the heart, and helps strengthen muscles and bones. But exercise is also good for the mind. Getting regular physical activity can boost mood and improve confidence. It can also be a great way to curb anxiety. For example, exercise helps keep the mind off those things that may cause anxiety and fear and boosts the availability of neurotransmitters, such a serotonin and GABA.

However, because exercise elevates the heart and breathing rate, it can cause a person to fear an oncoming panic attack. People who experience this so-called exercise-induced anxiety can engage in short bursts of exercise to help train the body and mind that heavy breathing and faster heart rate are not the enemy. The key is for people with panic disorder to take physical

Regular exercise can boost mood, improve confidence, and curb anxiety.

activity slow at first. If an elevated heart rate is a trigger for panic attacks, it is important to slowly train the brain to get used to those body signals. "The more you confront situations and symptoms that you perceive as threatening, the more you learn a new, non-threatening association in your brain," says L. Kevin Chapman, founder and director of the Kentucky Center for Anxiety and Related Disorders. "Once you recognize this necessary principle, physical exercise often becomes perceived as a strategy to relieve anxiety rather than a contributor to it."[32]

Katy, now a World Powerlifting Championship medalist, once suffered from frequent panic attacks. Her doctor prescribed medicine and exercise. She was terrified about going to a gym at first, but she went to different classes with a friend. "The difference it made to my mental health was incredible. My mood was much better, I had more energy. Eventually I came off my medication. . . . I have seen myself go from a withdrawn, anxious person to someone who is confident and happy."[33]

Deep Breathing

Learning deep-breathing and relaxation exercises is often a component of CBT. The patient uses these exercises to cope with situations that bring on fear, anxious feelings, or full-blown panic attacks.

Relaxation techniques can help calm the body and the mind. Recall that when panic comes on, it often increases the breathing rate and can cause a person to hyperventilate. This, in turn, can cause a person to become dizzy and light-headed and then possibly even more anxious. Learning to calm the breathing can help reduce these symptoms.

Most people do not think too much about their breathing and usually take short breaths instead of deep breaths. It takes practice to learn to breathe in a slower, more mindful way. Practicing at different times of day—when there are no symptoms of panic or anxiety—is key. This way, slowing down to breathe becomes more of a natural habit when panic symptoms arise.

With new technology come new ideas for treatment. Adi Wallach started having panic attacks while she was in college in Israel studying biomedical engineering. She says, "I was at the movies with friends the first time it happened. I felt my heart starting to race. Then I didn't feel my legs." Wallach went home and went to bed, hoping she would feel better in the morning. But she did not. She talked to her mom, who also happens to be a doctor. Her mom immediately recognized the signs of a panic attack. Wallach continued to have these attacks, sometimes six or seven times a day. She tried different approaches. "I changed my diet, started taking supplements, tried acupuncture. They were somewhat effective, but I was not able to use them fast enough to stop the attacks. I started avoiding places that might trigger an attack. I didn't go to the movies for years. I stopped swimming. I was afraid of flying."

Eventually, Wallach and her mom designed a device called CalmiGo. The handheld device looks like an asthma inhaler. It relies on vision, touch, and smell to regulate breathing, which in turn helps calm people in the throes of a panic attack.

Quoted in Brian Blum, "A New Handheld Device Aims to Calm Panic Attacks Fast," Israel21c, February 22, 2021. www.israel21c.org.

Slowing one's breathing involves inhaling slowly through the nose for a few seconds, holding that breath for a couple of seconds, and then exhaling slowly through the mouth for a few seconds. It sounds so simple, yet it takes concentration and patience.

J.T. had her first panic attack in a taxi. She suddenly could not breathe and felt crushing chest pain. She felt like she was dying. She went to see her doctor, who could find nothing wrong. A few weeks later, J.T. suffered another panic attack, this time on an airplane. Then the attacks happened more often. She started taking medicine to help with the symptoms she felt when an attack was imminent. But J.T. did not want to rely on medication, so she started meeting with a CBT therapist, who taught her strategies to get through attacks as they happened and to reduce the anxiety that triggered them. J.T. says that CBT was the key to getting her life back.

When J.T. feels a panic attack coming on, she focuses on her breathing. She takes deep breaths by inhaling deeply and exhaling slowly. She also may do something to interrupt the onset of the panic, such as put a cold washcloth on her face or spray her face with lavender water. She says it is important to acknowledge the oncoming symptoms and not fight them. "I remind myself that I am not dying. I am safe, and this will pass. In fact, each minute of the attack is bringing me closer to the end of it."[34]

Creating a Relaxing Space

Some people who have panic attacks find it helps to create a space designed for relaxation. Hazel had her first panic attack the day after a scary incident in her car. While driving at a high speed, she could not get the car to slow down. Although she figured out the problem and brought the car to a safe stop, the incident left her frazzled. A panic attack brought her to the emergency room, and she eventually developed panic disorder.

Hazel learned a lot about the value of relaxation and breathing techniques. She also discovered that creating relaxing spaces as retreats in the home can be helpful for dealing with anxiety. She soon got to work painting her bedroom and clearing it of clutter. "I now had a spot to retreat to when my anxiety levels soared. This, along with a relaxation technique I discovered, helped me feel as though I once again had control over my mind and body."[35]

Muscle Relaxation and Meditation

Progressive muscle relaxation is another technique used in CBT to help reduce stress and anxiety. The idea is that when the body is relaxed, it is hard to feel anxious. Like deep breathing, progressive muscle relaxation requires practice. The technique involves tensing a group of muscles while taking a deep breath in and relaxing those same muscles while letting that breath out.

The practice of meditation offers another way to reduce stress and calm anxiety, which makes it another helpful tool for people with panic disorder. Meditation is easy to learn, but it takes practice to truly reap the benefits.

Neal started to have panic attacks when he was thirty years old. He did everything he could to recover from the panic disorder and agoraphobia that had taken over his life. Finally, he discovered a treatment plan that worked: a combination of education and practice. First, he researched and learned all he could about panic attacks, panic disorder, and agoraphobia. Second, he learned and practiced both CBT and meditation. Neal says:

After my first two panic attacks, I awakened each morning to an instantly racing heart, hyperventilation, and cresting waves of fear and apprehension. My range of activity for each day was dictated by my agoraphobia, and my range gradually got narrower and narrower. . . . Every aspect of my life was deeply affected.

Panic disorder is in the mind, but it also very much in the body! . . . Through regular practice, I gradually learned to identify and then master each element of my panic response. . . . Through my practice of meditation, I learned to feel a sense of calm, safety, and well-being that I had never experienced before in my life.[36]

Smartphone Therapy

Technology has helped make mental health care more accessible to more people. For individuals with panic disorder who have been through CBT treatment, mobile mental health apps can provide support between sessions or after sessions have ended. According to the American Psychological Association, many of these apps can "help track symptoms, improve mood, evaluate the seriousness of the situation, or offer other insights in order to help users cope."[37]

Studies have found that this technology can help improve mental well-being and reduce psychological stress among adults. As a result of the COVID-19 pandemic, during which mental health needs grew but leaving home to seek help was problematic, more mental health apps have been developed. And they are catching on.

According to Stephen Schueller, executive director of the nonprofit One Mind PsyberGuide, ten thousand to twenty thousand mental health–related self-help apps are currently available to users. He predicts that many of these will not survive in the long run but says there are several that have good business plans and will continue to offer users mental health support.

These mental health apps offer deep-breathing training and other features. They offer sessions of five to ten minutes and have proved to help improve people's ability to cope in the face of stress and anxiety.

Not all apps are appropriate for use by someone with panic disorder. Anyone can develop an app and put it out there for people to use. Some may not be backed by the best science,

For individuals who have received cognitive behavioral therapy for panic disorder, mental health apps can provide support between therapy sessions.

and some people may be put off by therapy if they do not have a good experience. Users should be sure to speak with their mental health care provider for advice on which app might be the best fit.

Attaining Acceptance

For many people with panic disorder, the fear, anxiety, and attacks may never fully go away. The real goal of treatment is to be able to live with the disorder and to learn to cope when the heart starts to race, the palms start to sweat, and breathing is heavy and fast. Many people who have been able to learn about their condition and teach themselves coping mechanisms often speak of acceptance. They have accepted their condition and that panic attacks may happen. They have accepted that the attacks will end and that they will survive them. Most of all, though, these people have accepted that panic disorder will not define them. Panic will not keep them from living a full life. They have accepted that they can manage panic disorder instead of the other way around.

One person who sought treatment for panic disorder and found success says:

> Each and every time I talk about it, I feel less like an embarrassment and more like a hero. I don't say this to minimize the life-altering pain that panic disorder has caused me and will likely continue to cause me. I just hope that others know there's someone out there who shares your pain, who sees your pain and who truly believes that our pain makes us more—not less—worthy.[38]

Many people with panic disorder know that the condition will affect them for the rest of their lives, but they make lifestyle choices to take control of the condition. Gus took medication for his panic disorder before he decided he wanted to get off of it, and he has mostly kept the panic attacks at bay for years. He attributes his success to making lifestyle changes, including improving his diet, exercising, meditating, and getting a lot of CBT. But he also knows panic attacks will always be with him. Gus says:

> "I just hope that others know there's someone out there who shares your pain, who sees your pain and who truly believes that our pain makes us more—not less—worthy."[38]
>
> —Anonymous, a person who has panic disorder

> Certainly the experience of them was so intense that it feels almost that it's carved an indelible mark on my brain. It's not something that you forget in a hurry. I think they're always with you in a sense because however much you manage and you try to create a positive outlook, the fact is that it happened once and there's always a chance, however minor, that it might happen again. . . . So yes, they'll

very much always be with me. What I do feel, I feel an immense sense of achievement, having learnt how to bring them more under control.[39]

Getting control over the feelings of fear, anxiety, and panic is key to overcoming panic disorder. But it is also important for people with panic disorder to be kind to themselves, to forgive themselves if they start to revert to old thinking patterns. Managing and living with panic disorder can be challenging, but some with the disorder say it also has some positives. Annette is someone who feels this way. She explains, "Living with an anxiety disorder doesn't have to lessen your quality of life. You can get back all of the things you feel like you have lost. . . . In ways, anxiety offers its own gifts. It makes you vigilant about self-care, and demands that you pay attention to signs and symptoms. I'm more in tune with myself both emotionally and physically because of my anxiety."[40]

The Role of Nutrition

Studies have shown that what a person eats or does not eat can contribute to anxiety and other mental health disorders. Certain foods may help improve mood, increase energy, and calm the nervous system, while other foods may have the opposite effect.

Most mental health care providers advise their patients with panic disorder to limit or avoid alcohol and caffeine. While alcohol can initially make a person feel more relaxed, once that effect has worn off, it can cause people to feel uneasy. Caffeine elevates the heart rate and can make users feel nervous. Both substances can interfere with sleep.

Two nutrients that may play a role in panic attacks—especially in women—are iron and vitamin B_{12}. These nutrients help produce the neurotransmitter serotonin, which has a calming effect on the brain. Researchers have found that low levels of iron and vitamin B_{12} in the blood may contribute to panic attacks. Therefore, eating more foods that contain these nutrients might help with panic. Good sources of iron include dark-green leafy vegetables, such as kale; brown rice; nuts and seeds; fish; and tofu. Vitamin B_{12} is found in different kinds of fish, red meats, eggs, and yogurt.

Possibly one of the most important things to know, says a woman who has panic disorder, is that there is help for people with this disorder. Kathleen, who experienced her first panic attack on an airplane, says, "Anxiety can leave you feeling like you are merely existing . . . getting by, but not truly living. If you've been scared to reach out or open up about your struggles, I understand. But I can also promise you there is relief on the other side. The more we are open about our experiences, the more we open ourselves up to compassion, understanding, and a way forward."[41]

Introduction: Panic in Mid-Flight

1. Kathleen Munro, "Kathleen's Story: This Is How It Feels to Live with a Panic Disorder," Anxiety Canada, August 12, 2020. www.anxietycanada.com.
2. Munro, "Kathleen's Story."
3. Munro, "Kathleen's Story."
4. Munro, "Kathleen's Story."
5. Munro, "Kathleen's Story."

Chapter One: What Is Panic Disorder?

6. Katie, "Katie's Story: Recovering from Panic Attacks, Anxiety, and Depression," Mental Health Foundation, 2021. www.mentalhealth.org.uk.
7. Quoted in Mind, "Anxiety and Panic Attacks," 2021. www.mind.org.uk.
8. Quoted in Robin Wilder, "25 Stories of Panic Attacks and Living with Anxiety," BuzzFeed, August 24, 2014. www.buzzfeed.com.
9. Jenny Marie, "The Scariest Panic Symptoms People Don't Talk About," National Alliance on Mental Illness, December 4, 2018. www.nami.org.
10. Quoted in Substance Abuse and Mental Health Services Administration, "Impact of the DSM-IV to DSM-5 Changes on the National Survey on Drug Use and Health [Internet]," National Center for Biotechnology Information, 2016. www.ncbi.nlm.nih.gov.
11. Marie, "The Scariest Panic Symptoms People Don't Talk About."
12. Ellie, "Escaping My Agoraphobia," Mind, July 9, 2018. www.mind.org.uk.

Chapter Two: What Causes Panic Attacks and Panic Disorder?

13. Anonymous, "Awful Experiences—Age 15," Inner Health Studio, 2021. www.innerhealthstudio.com.

14. Quoted in Wilder, "25 Stories of Panic Attacks and Living with Anxiety."

15. Quoted in Wilder, "25 Stories of Panic Attacks and Living with Anxiety."

16. Quoted in NZCity, "Ella Henderson Was Hospitalized in Los Angeles After a Panic Attack," February 20, 2021. https://home.nzcity .co.nz.

17. Quoted in NZCity, "Ella Henderson Was Hospitalized in Los Angeles After a Panic Attack."

18. Quoted in Paul Li and Jeannine Stamatakis, "What Happens in the Brain When We Experience a Panic Attack?," *Scientific American*, July 1, 2011. www.scientificamerican.com.

19. Li and Stamatakis, "What Happens in the Brain When We Experience a Panic Attack?"

20. Nayla M. Khoury et al., "Interoception in Psychiatric Disorders: A Review of Randomized Controlled Trials with Interoception-Based Interventions," *Harvard Review of Psychiatry*, September–October 2018. www.ncbi.nlm.nih.gov.

21. Mohammed A. Memon, "What Are the Genetic Factors That Contribute to Panic Disorder?," Medscape, March 21, 2018. www .medscape.com.

22. Marie, "The Scariest Panic Symptoms People Don't Talk About."

23. Quoted in American Heart Association News, "AHA News: Anxiety Is Linked with Smoking—but How Is Still Hazy," *U.S. News & World Report*, January 22, 2021. www.usnews.com.

Chapter Three: Managing Panic Disorder

24. Quoted in National Alliance on Mental Illness, "Surviving Panic Disorder Is Something to Be Proud Of," 2021. www.nami.org.

25. American Psychological Association, "What Is Cognitive Behavioral Therapy?," 2017. www.apa.org.

26. Kristina Fenn and Majella Byrne, "The Key Principles of Cognitive Behavioural Therapy," *InnovAiT*, September 6, 2013. https://jour nals.sagepub.com.

27. A.T. Beck and D.J. Dozois, "Cognitive Therapy: Current Status and Future Directions," *Annual Review of Medicine*, 2011, p. 401.

28. American Psychological Association, "What Is Exposure Therapy?," 2017. www.apa.org.

29. Quoted in Mike Nichols, "Conquering Your Panic: Dave's Success Story," Anxiety, Panic & Health, January 8, 2009. https://anxiety panichealth.com.

30. Elli Thompson Purtell, "Why I Chose Anti-anxiety Medication," Huff-Post, December 6, 2017. www.huffpost.com.

Chapter Four: Living with Panic Disorder

31. Debra Kissen, "Losing and Finding My Mind: My Journey Through (and Most Days Past) Panic Disorder," HuffPost, October 14, 2014. www.huffpost.com.
32. Quoted in Jay Polish, "Experts Explain Why Exercising Sometimes Give You *More* Anxiety," Bustle, April 2, 2020. www.bustle.com.
33. Katy West, "From Panic Attacks to Powerlifts," Mind, March 4, 2016. www.mind.org.uk.
34. Quoted in Michelle Crouch, "This Is What a Panic Attack Feels Like," AARP, September 18, 2020. www.aarp.org.
35. Hazel Bennett, "Overcoming Panic Attacks with Relaxation Techniques," Resources to Recover, September 28, 2020. www.rtor.org.
36. Neal Sideman, "How I Achieved My Cure," Triumph over Panic, 2020. https://paniccure.com.
37. Nicole Owings-Fonner, "Choosing the Right CBT App for Depression and Anxiety," American Psychological Association, 2019. www.apaservices.org.
38. Quoted in National Alliance on Mental Illness, "Surviving Panic Disorder Is Something to Be Proud Of."
39. Quoted in Mind, "Mind Podcast—Anxiety and Panic Attacks," March 19, 2013. www.mind.org.uk.
40. Quoted in Wendy Rose Gould, "7 Steps for Getting Through a Panic Attack," NBC News, November 17, 2017. www.nbcnews.com.
41. Munro, "Kathleen's Story."

Getting Help and Information

American Academy of Child & Adolescent Psychiatry (AACAP)

www.aacap.org

A national professional medical association, the AACAP offers information to professionals, families, and young people about the mental health conditions that can affect children and adolescents, including panic disorder.

American Psychological Association

www.apa.org

This scientific and professional organization represents psychology in the United States. The association's website offers information about psychology topics, including panic disorder, for patients, loved ones, and researchers.

Anxiety & Depression Association of America (ADAA)

https://adaa.org

The ADAA works to prevent, treat, and cure anxiety disorders and depression. Its mission is to help improve the quality of life for people who have mental health disorders and their families with education, practice, and research. Its website offers a variety of educational resources and assistance in getting help for various mental health concerns.

Mental Health First Aid (MHFA)

www.mentalhealthfirstaid.org

The MHFA is a course that teaches people how to identify, understand, and respond to signs of mental illnesses and substance use disorders. Its website offers information on how to help people who experience panic attacks and other conditions. The "News and Updates" section of the website offers up-to-date information about panic disorder.

National Alliance on Mental Illness (NAMI)

www.nami.org

NAMI is a grassroots mental health organization dedicated to building better lives for Americans affected by mental illness. NAMI has local chapters nationwide. Its website offers education and support for people affected by mental health conditions, including patients, families, and loved ones.

National Institute of Mental Health (NIMH)

www.nimh.nih.gov

The NIMH is the US government's lead agency for research on mental health disorders. Its website offers information on a variety of topics related to mental health and the latest mental health research. The agency also offers information about clinical trials seeking participants to test new ways to prevent, detect, or treat mental illnesses.

Psych Central

www.psychcentral.com

Psych Central is an independent mental health news website that offers up-to-date information about mental health disorders, including panic disorder. Its goal is to help connect users with guidance and support to help make meaningful changes in their lives.

Books

Alexis Burling, *Understanding Panic Attacks*. San Diego, CA: Brightpoint, 2020.

Jennifer Conner-Smith, *Living with Panic Disorder*. San Diego, CA: ReferencePoint, 2018.

Regine Galanti, *Anxiety Relief for Teens: Essential CBT Skills and Mindfulness Practices to Overcome Anxiety and Stress*. New York: Penguin Random House, 2020.

Rachel Hutt, *Feeling Better: CBT Workbook for Teens: Essential Skills and Activities to Help Manage Moods, Boost Self-Esteem, and Conquer Anxiety*. Emeryville, CA: Althea, 2019.

Debra Kissen and Ashley D. Kendall, *Rewire Your Anxious Brain for Teens: Using CBT, Neuroscience, and Mindfulness to Help You End Anxiety, Panic, and Worry*. Oakland, CA: Instant Help, 2020.

Elena Welsh, *Cognitive Behavioral Therapy Workbook for Panic Attacks*. Emeryville, CA: Althea, 2019.

Internet Sources

Anxiety & Depression Association of America, "Panic Disorder," February 19, 2021. https://adaa.org.

Katie Hurley, "'What Does a Panic Attack Feel Like?' How to Explain a Panic Attack to a Loved One," Psycom, December 17, 2019. www.psycom.net.

Jenny Marie, "The Scariest Panic Symptoms People Don't Talk About," National Alliance on Mental Illness, December 4, 2018. www.nami.org.

Mental Health Foundation, "Katie's Story: Recovering from Panic Attacks, Anxiety, and Depression," 2021. www.mentalhealth.org.uk.

National Institute of Mental Health, "Panic Disorder," 2017. www.nimh .nih.gov.

Nicole Owings-Fonner, "Choosing the Right CBT App for Depression and Anxiety," American Psychological Association, 2019. www.apa services.org.

David Plans, "We've Lost Touch with Our Bodies," *Observations* (blog), *Scientific American*, February 5, 2019. https://blogs.scientificamerican .com.

Michael Stein, "Why Your Panic Attacks May Seem Random but Aren't," *Understanding the Anxious Mind* (blog), *Psychology Today*, February 11, 2021. www.psychologytoday.com.

Index

Cover: Athanasia Nomikou/Shutterstock

About the Author

Katie Sharp has been writing books for children and teens for many years. She lives in St. Louis, Missouri, with two dogs, two cats, and a revolving door of foster animals.